DANIEL BOONE

by Laura K. Murray

PEBBLE

a capstone imprint

Pebble Explore is published by Pebble, an imprint of Capstone.
1710 Roe Crest Drive
North Mankato, Minnesota 56003
www.capstonepub.com

Library of Congress Cataloging-in-Publication Data
Names: Murray, Laura K., author.
Title: Daniel Boone / Laura K. Murray.
Description: North Mankato, Minnesota : Pebble, an imprint of Capstone, [2021] | Series: Biographies | Includes bibliographical references and index. | Audience: Ages 6–8 | Audience: Grades 2–3 | Summary: "How much do you know about Daniel Boone? Find out the facts you need to know about this pioneer and explorer in early America. You'll learn about the early life, challenges, and major accomplishments of this famous American"—Provided by publisher.
Identifiers: LCCN 2020030661 (print) | LCCN 2020030662 (ebook) | ISBN 9781977132055 (hardcover) | ISBN 9781977133076 (paperback) | ISBN 9781977154071 (ebook)
Subjects: LCSH: Boone, Daniel, 1734–1820—Juvenile literature. | Explorers—Kentucky—Biography—Juvenile literature. | Pioneers—Kentucky—Biography—Juvenile literature. | Frontier and pioneer life—Kentucky—Juvenile literature. | Kentucky—Biography—Juvenile literature. | Cumberland Gap (Ky. and Va.)—Discovery and exploration—Juvenile literature. Classification: LCC F454.B66 M87 2021 (print) | LCC F454.B66 (ebook) | DDC 976.9/02092 [B]—dc23
LC record available at https://lccn.loc.gov/2020030661
LC ebook record available at https://lccn.loc.gov/2020030662

Image Credits

Alamy: Chronicle, 26, Pictures Now, 15; The Art Institute of Chicago: Karl Bodmer, Deliverance of the Daughters of Daniel Boone and Callaway, 1852, Gift of Dorothy Braude Edinburg to the Harry B. and Bessie K. Braude Memorial Collection, 19; iStockphoto: bauhaus1000, 22; Library of Congress: Photographs in the Carol M. Highsmith Archive, 16; Newscom: Ken Welsh, 21; North Wind Picture Archives: 5, 7, 8, 11, 12, 29, Gerry Embleton, 10; Science Source: 14; Shutterstock: Jim Vallee, 25, Nagel Photography, 23, Olena Rodina (geometric background), cover, back cover, 2, 29; Smithsonian Institution: National Portrait Gallery, partial gift of the William T. Kemper Foundation and of the Chapman Hanson Foundation, cover, 1, 20; Wikimedia: U.S. Navy, 24

Editorial Credits

Editor: Erika L. Shores; Designer: Elyse White; Media Researcher: Svetlana Zhurkin; Production Specialist: Spencer Rosio

Printed and bound in the USA.   3837

Table of Contents

Words in **bold** are in the glossary.

Who Was Daniel Boone?

Daniel Boone was a hunter and explorer. He led the way for people to move west during the 1700s. At that time, America was growing in size.

In Daniel's time, most white **settlers** lived on the East Coast. Daniel found new ways to go west. He made a path called the Wilderness Road. American Indians had lived on the land for many years.

There are many **folk stories** about Daniel. But not all of them are true.

Growing Up

Daniel was born November 2, 1734, in Berks County, Pennsylvania. Pennsylvania was one of the 13 **colonies** ruled by Great Britain.

Daniel was the sixth of 11 children. Growing up, he spent most of his time outside. He helped on the family's farm. He explored the woods. He went hunting and fishing. Daniel did not go to school. But his aunt taught him to read and write.

a colonial family by their log cabin in Pennsylvania

a hunter carrying home a turkey

Daniel was a good hunter. He learned to hunt with a long, pointed stick called a spear. Around age 12, his father gave him a rifle. Daniel hunted deer, turkeys, and other animals for his family to eat.

Daniel learned from the American Indians who lived nearby. They taught him about hunting and tracking animals. Around the time Daniel was 16, his family moved to North Carolina. The move took more than a year.

Fighting and Hunting

In 1754, the French and Indian War began. Daniel joined the North Carolina army. He and the colonists were on the side of the British. The French and some groups of American Indians were on the other side.

British soldiers and colonists fought French soldiers and American Indians in 1755.

Colonists worked on their small farms and hunted in the nearby woods.

After the war, Daniel went home to North Carolina. He married Rebecca Bryan on August 14, 1756. Daniel and Rebecca had 10 children. Daniel made money by hunting, trapping, and farming.

Settlers used rifles
to hunt wild animals.

Soon, problems started between the colonists and the Cherokee people. In 1759, the two groups fought. The Boones and other families moved to Virginia to stay safe. Daniel served in the North Carolina army during this time.

Three years later, the Boones went back to North Carolina. But it was hard for Daniel to earn money. Many new settlers had moved to the area. There were not as many animals left to hunt. Daniel looked for a new place to live. He traveled to Florida. But he decided not to move there.

Wilderness Road

In 1767, Daniel saw Kentucky for the first time. Kentucky was part of Virginia. The land was full of deer, bears, and other animals. Two years later, Daniel went to Kentucky again. Daniel and another hunter were captured by the Shawnee people. They told the hunters to never come back to their lands. Daniel did not listen.

The Shawnee captured Daniel and his friend.

Daniel and his family moved many times.

In 1773, the Boones and other families decided to move to Kentucky. On the way, American Indians fought to keep them out. Daniel's son James and others were killed. The families went back to North Carolina.

Daniel and his group arrived in Kentucky in 1775.

Settlers kept moving into the hunting lands of American Indians. In 1774, colonists and American Indians fought. Daniel was in charge of **forts** in Virginia. After the colonists won, they took over American Indian lands.

The next year, a company hired Daniel to make a trail into Kentucky. People wanted it to be a new colony. Boone led a team to clear a path through the Cumberland Gap. The path was called the Wilderness Road. It became a way for settlers to go west. Daniel's group also built a fort called Boonesborough.

Going West

Daniel was an army leader during the **Revolutionary War** (1775–1783). He and the colonists fought to be free from British rule.

In 1776, Cherokee and Shawnee Indians kidnapped Daniel's daughter Jemima and her two friends. Daniel helped rescue them. A few years later, Daniel was captured too. A Shawnee leader made him part of the tribe. But Daniel escaped.

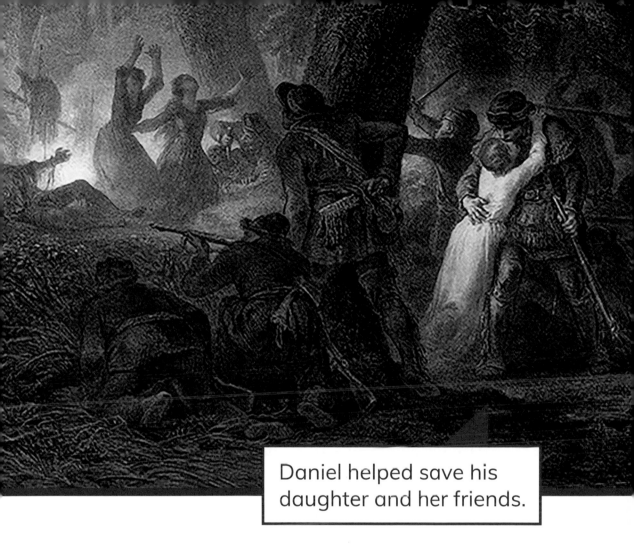

Daniel helped save his daughter and her friends.

During the war, Daniel also held **government** jobs. In 1782, he was made sheriff. The same year, Daniel's son Israel was killed in battle. America won the Revolutionary War in 1783.

In 1799, the Boones went farther west. Daniel was 65 years old. The family moved to Upper Louisiana. American Indians had lived there for many years. But the Spanish claimed the land as their own. By 1801, the land was owned by France.

In 1803, U.S. President Thomas Jefferson made a land deal with France. It was called the Louisiana Purchase. It nearly doubled the size of the country. The Boone family's land was part of the deal. Today, it is in Missouri.

Missouri was part of the Louisiana Purchase.

Daniel spent his later years with his family. He had money troubles. At times in his life, Daniel owned **enslaved** people. They were made to work without pay.

Daniel's grave in Kentucky

Daniel's son Nathan built a big house in Missouri. The family farmed, hunted, and grew food. Rebecca died in 1813. Daniel died on September 26, 1820. He was 85 years old.

Remembering Daniel

Today, some places in the United States are named for Daniel. Towns, schools, and parks have his name. There was a U.S. Navy submarine named after him.

The submarine USS *Daniel Boone* served from 1963 to 1984.

Daniel Boone National Forest

People can visit places from Daniel's life. The Daniel Boone National Forest is in Kentucky. People hike, hunt, and fish there. The Historic Daniel Boone Home is in Missouri. It is the home Nathan Boone built. Today, the Wilderness Road is part of U.S. Route 25.

Daniel became famous during his life. A book written in 1784 told about his adventures. People still tell stories about Daniel in books, movies, and poems. Some of the stories are tall tales. Many stories say Daniel wore a coonskin cap. But this is not true. Daniel liked to wear **felt** hats made out of beaver fur. They had wide brims.

Daniel Boone set out to explore new places. He had to solve problems on his own. He made new paths for others to follow. People will remember his love of adventure.

Important Dates

November 2, 1734	Daniel Boone is born in Berks County, Pennsylvania.
1750	Daniel's family moves to North Carolina.
1754	Daniel fights on the British side during the French and Indian War.
August 14, 1756	Daniel marries Rebecca Bryan.
1769	Daniel is captured by the Shawnee in Kentucky.
1775	Daniel helps clear a path to the west through the Cumberland Gap. It is called Wilderness Road.
1783	American colonies win the Revolutionary War against the British.
1799	Daniel and his family move to present-day Missouri.
1803	The Boones' Missouri land becomes part of the U.S. with the Louisiana Purchase.
September 26, 1820	Daniel dies in Missouri at age 85.

Fast Facts

Name:
Daniel Boone

Role:
explorer and hunter

Life dates:
November 2, 1734 to September 26, 1820

Key accomplishments:
Daniel Boone helped explore and settle parts of the American West. He helped make a trail called the Wilderness Road through the Cumberland Gap in the Appalachian Mountains. It became a main path people used to settle the West.

Glossary

colony (KAH-luh-nee)—an area that has been settled by people from another country and is owned by that country

enslave (en-SLAYV)—to make someone lose their freedom

felt (FELT)—a matted material

folk story (FOLK STOR-ee)—a legend or tale told and passed down from one group of people to the next

fort (FORT)—a place with strong walls where troops stay

Revolutionary War (rev-uh-LOO-shuhn-air-ee WOR)—the American colonies' fight from 1775 to 1783 for freedom from Great Britain

settler (SET-uh-lur)—a person who makes a home in a new place

Read More

Coutts, Lyn. *Explorers and Pioneers: Intrepid Adventurers Who Achieved the Unthinkable.* Hauppauge, NY: Barron's, 2018.

Raum, Elizabeth. *Cutting a Path: Daniel Boone and the Cumberland Gap.* North Mankato, MN: Capstone, 2016.

Internet Sites

Daniel Boone: PBS World Explorers
www.pbslearningmedia.org/resource/pbs-world-explorers-daniel-boone/

North Carolina Museum of History: Daniel Boone Legacy
www.ncmuseumofhistory.org/daniel-boone-legacy

The Historic Daniel Boone Home
www.sccmo.org/1701/The-Historic-Daniel-Boone-Home

Index